Edwin Waugh

Poems and Lancashire Songs

Second Edition

Edwin Waugh

Poems and Lancashire Songs
Second Edition

ISBN/EAN: 9783744712064

Printed in Europe, USA, Canada, Australia, Japan

Cover: Foto ©Thomas Meinert / pixelio.de

More available books at **www.hansebooks.com**

POEMS

AND LANCASHIRE SONGS.

BY

EDWIN WAUGH.

Second Edition.

LONDON:
WHITTAKER AND CO., AVE MARIA LANE.

MANCHESTER:
EDWIN SLATER, 16 ST. ANN'S SQUARE, AND
129 MARKET STREET.

1861.

PRINTED BY R. AND R. CLARK, EDINBURGH.

To John Bright.

CONTENTS.

POEMS.

	Page
The Moorland Flower	1
Time is Flying	5
The Moorlands	8
To the Rose-tree on My Window-sill	11
Keen Blows the North Wind	21
The Captain's Friends	24
Now Summer's Sunlight Glowing	29
The World	34
To a Married Lady	38
Cultivate your Men	40
Old Man's Song	43
Bide on	46
The Moorland Witch	48
The Church Clock	51
God Bless Thee, Old England	53
Christmas Song	55

Contents.

	Page
Love and Gold	58
All on a Rosy Morn of June	63
Glad Welcome to Morn's Dewy Hours	66
Alas! how Hard it is to Smile	68
Ye Gallant Men of England	70
Here's to my Native Land	73
What makes your Leaves fall down?	76
When Drowsy daylight	78
Mary	80
Oh! had she been a Lowly Maid	82
The Old Bard's Welcome Home	84
Oh! come across the Fields	87
Oh! Weave a Garland for my Brow	90
To the Spring Wind	92
Nightfall	94
To a Young Lady	97
Poor Travellers All	99
The Dying Rose	103
Lines	107
The Man of the Time	10
The Wanderer's Hymn	111
Alone, upon the Flowery Plain	113
Life's Twilight	115
Christmas Morning	118

Contents.

SONGS
IN THE LANCASHIRE DIALECT.

	Page
Come Whoam to thy Childer an' me	125
What ails Thee, my Son Robin?	129
God Bless these Poor Folk	132
Come, Mary, Link thi Arm i' mine	136
Chirrup	140
The Dule's i' this Bonnet o' mine	144
Tickle Times	147
Jamie's Frolic	151
Owd Pinder	157
Come, Jamie, let's undo thi Shoon	160
Th' Goblin Parson	163
While takin' a Wift o' my Pipe	168
God bless thi Silver Yure!	171
Margit's Comin'	176

THE MOORLAND FLOWER.

I.

BENEATH a crag, whose forehead rude
    O'erfrowns the mountain side,—
Stern monarch of the solitude,
    Dark-heaving, wild, and wide,—
A floweret of the moorland hill
    Peeped out unto the sky,
In a mossy nook, where a limpid rill
    Came tinkling blithely by.

II.

Like a star-seed, from the night-skies flung
    Upon the mountains lone,
Into a gleaming floweret sprung,—
    Amid the wild it shone;
And bush and brier, and rock and rill,
    And every wandering wind,
In interchange of sweet good-will
    And mutual love did bind.

III.

In the gloaming grey, at close of day,
    Beneath the deepening blue,
It lifted up its little cup,
    To catch the evening dew:—
The rippling fall, the moorfowl's call,
    The wandering night-wind's moan;
It heard, it felt, it loved them all,—
    That floweret sweet and lone.

IV.

The green fern wove a screening grove
    From noontide's fervid ray;
The pearly mist of the brooklet kist
    Its leaves with cooling spray;
And, when dark tempests swept the waste,
    And north winds whistled wild,
The brave old rock kept off the shock,
    As a mother shields her child.

V.

And when it died the south wind sighed,
    The drooping fern looked dim;
The old crag moaned, the lone ash groaned,
    The wild heath sang a hymn;
The leaves crept near, though fallen and sere,
    Like old friends mustering round;
And the dew-drop fell from the heather-bell
    Upon its burial ground.

VI.

For it had bloomed content to bless
    Each thing that round it grew;
And on its native wilderness
    Its store of sweetness strew:
Fair link in nature's chain of love,
    To noisy fame unknown,
There is a register above,
    E'en when a flower is gone.

VII.

So, lovingly embrace thy lot,
    Though lowly it may be,
And beautify the little spot
    Where God hath planted thee:
To win the world's approving eyes
    Make thou no foolish haste,—
Heaven loves the heart that lives and dies
    To bless its neighbouring waste.

TIME IS FLYING.

I.

TIME is flying!
Are we hieing
To a brighter, better bourne?
Or, unthinking,
Daily sinking
Into night that knows not morn?

II.

Oh, what is life
But duty's strife?
A drill; a watchful sentry's round;
A brief campaign
For deathless gain;
A bivouac on battle-ground:

III.

An arrow's flight;
A taper's light;
A fitful day of sun and cloud;
A flower; a shade;
A journey made
Between a cradle and a shroud.

IV.

Oh, what is death?
A swordless sheath;
A jubilee; a mother's call;
A kindly breast,
That offers rest
Unto the poorest of us all;

V.

The wretched's friend;
Oppression's end;
The outcast's shelter from the cold;

To regions dim,
The portal grim
Where misers leave their loads of gold;

VI.

A voyage o'er;—
A misty shore,
With time-wrecked generations strown;
Where each mad age
Has spent its rage
Upon a continent unknown

THE MOORLANDS.

I.

SING hey for the moorlands, wild, lonely, and stern,
 Where the moss creepeth softly all under the fern;
Where the heather-flower sweetens the lone highland
 lea,
And the mountain winds whistle so fresh and so free!

I've wandered o'er landscapes embroidered with flowers,
The richest, the rarest, in greenest of bowers,
Where the throstle's sweet vesper, at summer day's
 close,
Shook the coronal dews on the rim of the rose;
But oh for the hills where the heather-cock springs
From his nest in the bracken, with dew on his wings!
 Sing, hey for the moorlands?

II.

I've lingered by streamlets that water green plains,
I've mused in the sunlight of shady old lanes,
Where the mild breath of evening came sweetly and slow
From green nooks where bluebells and primroses grow;
But oh the bold hills that look up at the skies,
Where the green brackens wave to the wind as it flies!
    Sing, hey for the moorlands!

III.

Away with the pride and the fume of the town,
And give me a lodge in the heatherland brown;
Oh there, to the schemes of the city unknown,
Let me wander with freedom and nature, alone;
Where wild hawks with glee on the hurricane sail,
And the rough crags delight in the rush of the gale
    Sing, hey for the moorlands!

IV.

In glens which resound to the waterfall's song,
My spirit should play, the wild echoes among:
I'd climb the dark steep to my lone mountain home,
And, heartsome and poor, o'er the solitude roam:
And the keen winds that harp on the heathery lea
Should sing the grand anthem of freedom to me!
      Sing, hey for the moorlands!

TO

THE ROSE-TREE ON MY WINDOW-SILL.

1.

DARK is the lot of him with heart so dull
  By sensual appetite's unbridled sway,
As to be blind unto the beautiful
  In common things that strew the common way.
Trailing the dusty elements of death,
  He crawls, in his embruted blindness, proud;
To perishable ends he draws his breath;
  His life, a funeral passing through a crowd;
His soul, a shrunken corpse within; his body, but a
    shroud.

II.

Nature! kind handmaid of the thoughtful soul,
    Be thy sweet ministrations ever mine;
Thy angel-influences keep me whole,
    And lead my spirit into things divine:
Holding thy lovely garment, when a child,
    I walked in simple ecstasy with thee;
And now, with sadder heart, and travel-toiled,
    Thou hast a sanctuary still for me,
Where oft I find repose from earthly care and misery.

III.

In cities proud, by grovelling factions torn,
    Where glittering pomp and stony-eyed despair,
Murder and stealth, the lordly and the lorn,
    Squalor and wealth, divide the Christian air;—
Where prowling outcasts hug with ignorant rage
    Some sense of wrong that smoulders deep within;—

Where mean intrigues their furtive battles wage;
　Where they are wrong that lose, and they are
　　right that win,—
And drowning virtue struggles with the waves of
　sin;—

IV.

Where drooping penitence, and pious pride;
　The sons of labour and the beasts of prey;
The spoilers and the spoiled, are side by side,
　Jostling unkindly on the crowded way;—
E'en there sweet Nature sings her heaven-taught
　songs,—
Unheeded minstrel of the fuming street,—
For ever wooing its discordant throngs
　With sounds and shapes that teem with lessons
　　meet,—
Like thee, fair rose-tree, on my window blooming
　sweet.

V.

Oh, floral comrade of my lonely hours,
    Sweet soother of my saddest mood,
The summer's glow, the scents of summer flowers,
    Are filling all my solitude:
The thick-leaved groves, whose sylvan rooflets ring
    With blending lyrics poured from every tree,
The sleepy streams where swallows dip the wing,
    The wild flowers, nodding in the wind, I see,—
And hear the murmurous music of the roving bee.

VI.

Taking my willing fancy by the hand,
    Thou leadest me through nature like a child,
Where rustling forests robe the pleasant land,
    And lonely streamlets ripple through the wild;—
Through verdant nooks, where, on the long, cool grass
    The lingering dews light up the leafy shade,
In dreamy bliss, my wandering footsteps pass,
    Sweeping from many a lush and bending blade
The load of liquid pearls that such a twinkling made.

VII.

Now, through a sunny glade, away, away,—
    Oh, let me wander thus a while with thee,—
By many a pleasant streamlet we will play,
    And gad o'er many a field in careless glee:
Thus gently thou, when on life's pathway rude
    My heart grows faint as gloomy shadows lower,
Leadest me back into a happier mood,
    By some sweet, secret, heaven-inspired power,
That lurks in thy fringed leaf and orient-tinted flower.

VIII.

My spirit bursts its prison-house of care,
    And dreamily, with lingering feet, I stray
Where garden odours fill the golden air,
    And blossoms tremble to the wild birds' lay;—
O'er cool moist slopes, beneath the woodland shade,
    Where the blithe throstle in his chamber sings,
Then wonders at the music he has made;—
    Where the lush bluebell's little censer swings,
And pleasant incense to the wandering breezes flings.

IX.

Upon a shady bank, as I recline,
    Gazing, with silent joy, the landscape o'er,
I feel its varied glories doubly mine—
    My heart's inheritance, my fancy's store;
Above me waves a roof of green and gold—
    Delightful shelter from the noontide heat;
Beyond, a wandering streamlet I behold,
    Where wind and sunlight on the waters meet
In silvery shimmerings, past description sweet.

X.

I hear the skylark, poised on trembling wings,
    Teaching the heavenly quire his thrilling lay,
All nature seems to listen as he sings,
    Hushed into stillness by his minstrelsy;—
As the blithe lyric streams upon the lea,
    Steeping the wild flowers in melodious rain,
The very dewdrops, dancing to the glee,
    Look up with me, but, like me, look in vain
To find the heaven-hid singer of that matchless strain.

XI.

Now, on rough byways, sauntering through the sun,
   From fertile haunts of man I gladly stray,
Up to the sweet brown moorlands, bleak and dun,
   While rindling waters tinkle o'er my way;
Where the free eagle lords it in the sky;
   Where red grouse, springing from the heath'ry steep,
Wake the wild echoes with their lonely cry;
   And whistling breezes unrestrainèd sweep
O'er the old hills, that in the sunlight seem asleep.

XII.

O'er yon wild height, between the rugged steeps,
   From crag to crag, in many an airy bound
Of mighty glee, the mountain torrent leaps,
   And the lone ravine trembles to the sound;
Through cave and cleft, along the narrow glen,
   The rushing thunders rage, and roll afar,
Like untamed lions struggling in their den,—
   With unavailing rage,—each rocky scar
Hurls back the prisoned roar of elemental war.

XIII.

As homeward, down a winding path I stray,
 Where mazy midges in the twilight throng,
In plaintive fits of liquid melody,
 I hear the lonely ousel's vesper-song;
Odours of unseen flowers the air pervade;
 As I sit listening on a wayside mound,
Watching the daylight and its business fade,
 The evening stillness fills with weird sound,
And distant waters sing their ancient choral round.

XIV.

Mild evening brings the gauzy fringe of dreams
 That trails upon the golden skirts of day;
And here and there a cottage candle gleams
 With cheerful twinkle o'er my drowsy way;
As flaxen-headed elves, from rambles wild,
 With straggling footsteps, to their mothers hie
With woodland trophies, and with garments soiled,

All tired and pleased,— they know not, care not why;—
So from my wand'rings I return, as daylight quits the sky.

XV.

Oh, flowery leader of these fancy flights,
    Epitome of Nature's charms to me,
Filling my spirit with such fine delights
    As I can never more repay to thee,—
For my behoof thou donn'st the summer's sheen,
    Smiling benignly on thy prison-spot,
Though exiled from that native nook of green
    Where playmate zephyrs seek through bower and grot,
Through all the summer roses seek, but find thee not.

XVI.

Fair lamp of beauty, in my cloistral shade,
    Though brief at best the time thou hast to shine,
By an almighty artist thou wert made,
    And touched with light eternally divine.

Like a caged bird, in this seclusion dim,—
    Where slanting sunbeams seldom find a way,—
Singing with patient joy a silent hymn,
    That wafts my thought from worldly care away
Into the realms of Nature's endless holiday.

XVII.

Sweet specimen of Nature's mystic skill,
    Dost thou know aught of human joys and woes?
Can'st thou be gladdened by the glad heart's thrill,
    Or feel the writhing spirit's silent throes?
To me thou art a messenger of love—
    A leaf of peace amid the storms of woe—
Dropt in my path by that celestial Dove
    Who made all things in heaven and earth below,
That wandering man the beautiful and true might know.

KEEN BLOWS THE NORTH WIND.

I.

KEEN blows the north wind; the woodlands are bare;
 The snow-shroud lies white on the flowerless lea;
The red-breast is wailing the death of the year,
 As he cowers his wing in the frozen haw-tree.

II.

The leaves of the forest, now summer is o'er,
 Lie softly asleep in the lap of decay;
And the wildflower rests on the snow-covered shore,
 Till the cold night of winter has wandered away.

III.

Oh, where are the small birds that sang in yon bowers
    When last summer smiled on the green-mantled plain?
Oh, where do they shelter in winter's bleak hours?
    Will they come back with spring, to delight me again?

IV.

But I may be gone, never more to behold
    The wildflowers peep, when the winter has fled;
The chill drifts of sorrow the wanderer may fold,
    And the sunshine of spring melt the snow on his bed.

V.

But come, ye sweet warblers, and sport in the spray,
    Whose tender revival I never may see;
The young buds will leap to your welcoming lay,—
    'T will cheer the sad-hearted, as oft it cheered me.

VI.

And should ye, returning, then find me at rest,
    Stay sometimes, and sing near the grave of a friend;
Drop a rosemary leaf on his turf-covered breast,
    And rejoice that his troublesome journey's at end.

THE CAPTAIN'S FRIENDS.

1.

I WANDERED down by yonder park one quiet autumn day,
When many a humble traveller was going on the way;
And there I saw a company of neighbours great and small,
All gathered round an ancient gate that leads unto the hall.

II.

The faded leaves that rustled in the mournful autumn wind
Awoke in me a train of thought that saddened all my mind;
And through the crowd of anxious folk there went a smothered wail,
So I sat me down upon a stone and hearkened to the tale.

III.

The sturdy farmer from his fields had hurried to the place,
The cripple on his crutches, and the sick with pallid face;
The poor old dame had wandered with her blind man to the ground,
And the lonely widow, weeping, with her children gathered round.

IV.

The well-remembered beggar, too, was there — but not
    to beg;
And the stiff old Chelsea pensioner, upon a wooden
    leg:
From hamlet, fold, and lonely cot the humble poor
    were there,
Each bringing in his moistened eye a tributary tear.

V.

Up spake the sturdy farmer to the porter, and he
    said,
"What news is this that's going round? They say
    the Captain's dead!"
The quaint old porter laughed, "Aha! Thank God,
    it isn't true!
It's but the Captain's dog that's dead — they called it
    'Captain' too!"

VI.

Then sprang the cripple on his crutch, and nearly came
    to ground;
The blind man wandered to and fro, and shook their
    hands all round;
The dame took snuff, the sick man smiled, and blest
    the happy day;
And the widow kissed her young ones, as she wiped
    their tears away.

VII.

Up rose the children's voices, mingling music with the
    gale,
And the begger's dog romped with them, as he barked
    and wagged his tail;
The farmer snapt his thumbs, and cried, "Come on, I'll
    feast you all!"
And the stark old soldier with his stick kept charging
    at the wall.

VIII.

So, now the Captain's dog is dead and sleeping in the ground,
A kind old master by the grave bemoans his gallant hound;
He says, "My hair is white and thin! I have not long to stay!
And, oh, my poor old dog, how I shall miss thee on the way!"

IX.

Then here's to every noble heart that's gentle, just, and brave,
That cannot be a tyrant, and that grieves to see a slave.
God save that good old Captain long, and bring his soul to joy;—
The countryside will lose a friend the day he comes to die.

NOW SUMMER'S SUNLIGHT GLOWING.

1.

NOW, summer's sunlight glowing,
    Streaks the woodland shade with gold;
And balmy winds are blowing
    Softly o'er the moorland-wold;
Now sweet smells the bluebell,
    'Neath the valley's leafy screen;
And thick grows the wild rose,
    Clust'ring o'er the hedges green.

The green fern waves upon the steep;
   The smiling fields are flowered o'er;
And modest little daisies peep
   Like children at a mother's door!

II.

From dewy meadows springing,
   Yonder blinding skies among,
The poet-lark is singing,
   As if his heart was made of song!
While gladly and madly
   In every grove the wild birds vie,
All tingling and mingling
   In tipsy routs of lyric joy!
My throbbing heart with every part
   Is dancing to the chorus near,—
The gush, the thrill,—the wizard trill—
   Like drops of water tinkling clear!

III.

The cottage matron, knitting
    In her little garden, sings,
As wild birds, round her flitting,
    Fan the blossom with their wings;
And twining, combining,
    The honeysuckle and the rose,
Sweet shading, and braiding,
    Round her winking lattice goes;
And wild bees through the flowers roam—
    The little happy buzzing thieves!—
Here and there, with busy hum,
    Rifling all the honeyed leaves.

IV.

Now, hamlet urchins roaming,
    All the sunny summer day,
From dewy morn till gloaming,
    Through the rustling wildwood stray;

There blithely and lithely,
    By warbling brook and sylvan grot,
They ramble and gambol,
    All the busy world forgot;—
Like birds that wing the sunny air,
    And warble in the tangled wild,
Unhaunted by the dreams of care,—
    Oh, to be again a child!

V.

Sweet scents and sunshine blending;
    The wildwoods, in their leafy pride,
To the gentle south wind bending;—
    Oh, the bonny summer tide!
The tinkling, the twinkling,
    Where little limpid rivers lave;
The sipping, the dipping
    Of wildflowers in the gilded wave;—

Now Summer's Sunlight.

The fruitful leas, the blooming trees,
    The pleasant fields, embroidered fair;
The wild birds' little melodies,
    Scattering gladness everywhere!

THE WORLD.

I.

THIS foolish world doth wink
    Its cunning lid;
And, when it thinks, it thinks
    Its thoughts are hid.

II.

Its piety's a screen
    Where vice doth hide;
Its purity's unclean;
    Its meekness, pride.

III.

Its charity's a bait
   To catch a name;
Its kindness covers hate;
   Its praise is blame.

IV.

Its wisdom soweth seeds
   Which follies prove;
And its repentance needs
   Repenting of.

V.

Its learning's empty talk;
   Its heart is cold;
Its church is an exchange;
   Its god is gold.

VI.

Its pleasures all are blind,
   And lead to pain;
Its treasures are a kind
   Of losing gain.

VII.

Lust moves it more than love,
    Fear more than shame;
Its best ambitions have
    A grovelling aim.

VIII.

Its laws are a disgrace;
    Its lords are slaves;
Its honours are misplaced,
    E'en on our graves.

IX.

Some sorrow doth attend
    Its happiest dreams;
And rottenness doth end
    Its rotten schemes.

X.

Oh, cure our moral madness—
    Our soul-disease;
Shew us that Vice brings sadness,
    And Virtue, ease.

The World.

XI.

And teach us in the hour
Of Sin's dismay,
That Truth's the only flower
Without decay.

TO A MARRIED LADY.

I.

AH, this wild voyage o'er the sea of life
    Needs all the help that heaven to earth can give;
Through its dark storms and shoals and battle-strife
    God must be pilot to the ships that live.

II.

Happy the heart that finds a haven of love
    Where in the tempest it can sweetly moor,
And taste below the bliss that but above
    Is ever stainless, and is ever sure.

III.

And blest the hearth where pure affections glow—
    The husband's and the father's best retreat;
Where heavenward souls in one direction grow,
    With darling tendrils round them twining sweet.

IV.

Such be thy home; through earth's mutations strange,
  A garden, where the flowers of heaven grow;
And, sheltered there from blight, through every change,
  Its loves, its hopes, no touch of ruin know.

V.

May Time, whose withering finger ever brings,
  To Nature's best the doom of sure decline,
Float over thee with gently-fanning wings,
  And find the twilight of thy life divine.

VI.

And, ever hand in hand along your path,
  For thee and thine thus doth the poet pray,
That ye may walk in joy from life to death,
  And earth's night be the dawn of heaven's day.

CULTIVATE YOUR MEN.

I

TILL as ye ought your barren lands,
    And drain your moss and fen;
Give honest work to willing hands,
    And food to hungry men;
And hearken—all that have an ear—
    To this unhappy cry,—
"Are poor folk's only chances here
    To beg, to thieve, or die?"

II.

With kindly guerdon this green earth
    Rewards the tiller's care,
And to the wakening hand gives forth
    The bounty slumbering there;

But there's another, nobler field
    Big with immortal gain,—
The morasses of mind untilled;—
    Go,—cultivate your men!

III.

Oh, ponder well, ye pompous men
    With Mammon-blinded eyes,
What means the poverty and pain
    That moaning round you lies;
And plough the wastes of human mind
    Where weedy ignorance grows,—
These baleful deserts of mankind
    Would blossom like the rose.

IV.

But penny-wise, pound-foolish thrift
    Deludes this venal age;
Blind self's the all-engrossing drift,
    And pelf, the sovereign rage.

E'en in the Church the lamp grows dim,
    That ought to light to heaven,
And that which fed its holy flame,
    To low ambition's given.

v.

Just retribution hovers near
    This play of pride and tears;
To heaven all worldly cant is clear,
    Whatever cloak it wears;
And high and low are on a path
    That leads into the grave,
Where false distinctions flit from death,
    And tyrant rots with slave.

OLD MAN'S SONG.

1.

OH! sweetly the morning of childhood
    Awoke me to careless delight;
And blithe as a bird of the wildwood
    I played in its beautiful light;
The world was a magical treasure
    That filled me with wonder and joy;
And I fluttered from pleasure to pleasure,
    Delighted—I couldn't tell why:
        If I thought of to-morrow,
        I dreamt not of sorrow;
    And I smiled as the day went by.

II.

Gay youth, with its glittering hours,
    Came frolicking on, full of glee,
Where hope's charming sunlighted bowers
    Were thickly in blossom for me;—
My heart was a harp whose emotion
    Awoke to all beautiful things,
And love was the dearest devotion
    That played in its tremulous strings:
        So, I dallied, delighted,
        And carelessly slighted
Old Time and his rustling wings.

III.

Now, the noontide of life has gone by me,
    The visions of morning have died;
And the world is beginning to try me
    With struggles that chasten my pride;—

Old Man's Song.

As the twilight of time, softly stealing,
    Comes o'er me with shadows of grey,
I feel the sad truth now revealing,—
    It draws to the close of the day;
        And thoughtfully eyeing
        The past, I sit sighing,
And wondering how long I shall stay.

BIDE ON.

I.

WHEN thy heart 'neath its trouble sinks down,
    And the joys that misled it are gone,—
When the hopes that inspired it are flown,
    And it gropes in the darkness alone,—
        Let faith be thy cheer,
        Scorn the whispers of fear,
Be righteous, and bravely bide on.

II.

When fancy's wild meteor-ray
    Allures thee from duty to roam,
Beware its bewildering way,
    And rest with thy conscience at home;—
        Give ear to its voice;
        Let the stream of thy joys
From the fountain of purity come.

III.

When, by failure and folly borne down,
    The future looks hopelessly drear,
And each day, as it flies, with a frown,
    Tells how helpless, how abject we are;
        Let nothing dismay
        Thy bold effort to-day;—
Be patient, and still persevere.

IV.

Be steady, in joy and in sorrow;
    Be truthful, in great and in small;
Fear nothing but sin, and each morrow
    Heaven's blessing upon thee shall fall:
        In thy worst tribulation
        Shun low consolation,
And trust in the God that sees all.

THE MOORLAND WITCH.

1.

THERE lives a lass on yonder moor—
  She wears a gown of green;
She's handsome, young, and sprightly,
  With a pair of roguish een:
She's graceful as the mountain doe
  That snuffs the forest air;
And she brings the smell of the heather-bell
  In the tresses of her hair.

II.

'Twas roaming careless o'er the hills,
    As sunlight left the sky,
That first I met this moorland maiden
    Bringing home her kye:
Her native grace, her lovely face,
    The pride of art outshone;—
I wondered that so sweet a flower
    Should blossom thus alone.

III.

Alas, that ever I should meet
    Those beaming eyes of blue,
That round about my thoughtless heart
    Their strong enchantment threw.
I could not dream that falsehood lurked
    In such an angel smile;
I could not fly the fate that lured
    With such a lovely wile.

IV.

And when she comes into the vale,
    To try her beauty's power,
She'll leave a spell on many a heart
    That fluttered free before.
But, oh, beware her witching smile,—
    'Tis but a fowler's snare;
She's fickle as the mountain wind
    That frolics with her hair!

THE CHURCH CLOCK.

I.

OH thou, who dost these pointers see,
    And hear'st the chiming hour,
Say, do I tell the time to thee,
    And tell thee nothing more;—
I bid thee mark life's little day
    By strokes of duty done;—
A clock may stop at any time,
    But time will travel on.

II.

I am a preacher to a few,
    A servant unto all,
As here I stand tick, ticking,
    Like a death-watch in a wall;
And, it were well that those who see
    These fingers gliding on,
Should think a moment, now and then,
    How fast the moments run.

III.

There's some of you are wealthy,
    And some of you are proud,
And some are poor, and some are sad,
    And waiting for a shroud;—
Be patient yet a while, for see
    This little yard below,—
The man who goes the longest way,
    Has not so far to go.

IV.

A christ'ning; then, a wedding comes;
    And then, a passing bell;
'T is just the ancient tale that time
    Has always had to tell:
The very clock that marks the hour,
    With ticking wears away;
The gladdest pulse of life contains
    The music of decay.

GOD BLESS THEE, OLD ENGLAND!

I.

GOD bless thee, old England, the home of the free;
    A garden of roses, begirt by the sea!
The wild waves that fondle thy darling green shore
Shall sing thy proud story till time be no more;
And nations unborn, looking over the wave,
Shall tell of the isle of the free and the brave,
Where liberty's battle, through ages of old,
Was fought in the hearts of the just and the bold;—
    Old England, the Queen of the Sea!

II.

May truth ever flourish thy children among;
And deeds that awaken the spirit of song
Inspire future bards with emotion divine,
Till earth has no anthem so noble as thine!
Green cradle of manliness, beauty, and worth!
May thy name be a watchword of joy in the earth
When I have long mouldered beneath the green sod,—
A country devoted to freedom and God;—
   Old England, the Queen of the Sea!

CHRISTMAS SONG.

I.

IN the dark-clouded sky no star shews a gleam;
    The drift-laden gale whistles wild in the tree;
The ice-mantle creeps o'er the murmuring stream,
    That glittering runs through the snow-covered lea;
But, hark! the old bells fling the news to the wind!—
    Good Christians awake to their genial call;—
The gale may blow on, we'll be merry and kind;—
    Blithe yule and a happy new year to us all!
        Bring in the green holly, the box and the yew,
            The fir and the laurel, all sparkling with rime;
        Hang up to the ceiling the mistletoe-bough,
            And let us be jolly another yule-time!

II.

While, garnished with plenty, together we meet,
    In carolling joy, as the glad moments flee,
Thus sheltered away from the frost and the sleet,
    With friends all around us in festival glee,
We'll still keep the heavenly lesson in mind,—
    A gentle Redeemer was born at this tide;
The wind may blow keenly, but we will be kind,
    And think of the poor folk that shiver outside.
        Bring in the green holly, the box and the yew,
            The fir and the laurel, all sparkling with rime;
        Hang up to the ceiling the mistletoe-bough,
            And let us be jolly another yule time!

III.

He's a cur who can bask in the fire's cheery light,
    And hearken, unheeded, the winter wind blow,
And care not a straw for the comfortless wight
    That wanders about in the frost and the snow;

But we'll think of the mournful the while we are glad;
Our hearts shall be kind as the winter is keen;
And we'll share our good cheer with the poor and the sad,
That sorrow and struggle in corners unseen.
    Bring in the green holly, the box and the yew,
      The fir and the laurel, all sparkling with rime;
    Hang up to the ceiling the mistletoe-bough,
    And let us be jolly another yule time!

LOVE AND GOLD.

I.

WE were but poor young people,
    My Margaret and I;
And well I knew she loved me,
    Although her looks were shy:
But I longed to see strange countries,
    That lie beyond the main;
And when I'd gathered riches,
    Come flaunting home again.

II.

When I parted from my true love,
    A rover's fate to try,
She was full of strange forebodings,
    And tears were in her eye.
Pale looks of silent sorrow
    She gave to all my glee,
When I said, "I'll win some gold, love,
    And bring it back to thee!"

III.

But my heart was proudly beating,
    And I was in my prime,
So, in chase of golden treasure,
    I went from clime to clime;
In giddy chase of pleasure,
    Beyond the foaming sea,
All heedless of the maiden
    Who pined at home for me.

IV.

So I sought for gold, and won it,
    And still I wanted more,
And as my treasure gathered,
    Was poorer than before:
For it made me proud and heartless;
    It made me hard and cold;
It made me slight my true love—
    That cursèd yellow gold!

V.

But, in spite of all my riches,
    I was growing old and worn,
So I took a ship for England,
    The place where I was born;
I took a ship for England,
    With all my golden store,
To dazzle those that knew me
    Full thirty years before.

VI.

When I landed with my gold-bags,
   The friends of old were gone;
And, in spite of all my riches,
   I felt myself alone.
Though strangers fluttered round me
   I knew their hearts were cold;
And I sought in vain the true love,
   That's never bought with gold.

VII.

My skin was parched and yellow,
   My hair was thin and grey,
And she that loved me dearly,
   Was sleeping in the clay.
She had long been in the churchyard,
   Sleeping sweet and sound;—
And I was but an outcast
   Upon the lonely ground.

VIII.

Now to her grave I wander,
 And sit upon the stone,
Where all is still and silent,—
 Except my lonely moan;
But I shall soon be going,
 For I am ill and old;
And my gold will deck the mourners,
 Who wish my body cold.

ALL ON A ROSY MORN OF JUNE.

I.

ALL on a rosy morn of June,
    When farmers make their hay,
Down by yon bonny woodland green
    A milking maid did stray;
And oh, but she was sweet and fair,—
    The flower of all the vale;
In her hand a wild white rose she bare,
    And on her head a pail.

II.

Across the fields, as she did rove,
    The pretty maiden sang
A plaintive lay of tender love,
    That through the valley rang:
Blithe as a linnet on the spray,
    Among the wildwood green,
She lilted on her flowery way,—
    And vanished from the scene.

III.

When next I saw that pleasant vale—
    Twelve moons had wandered by—
A matron told her hapless tale
    With tear-drops in her eye;
For there had been, with winsome wile,
    A careless-hearted lad,
And plucked the flower whose lovely smile
    Made all the valley glad.

IV.

The woods were gay and green again;
　The sun was smiling on;
But the charmer of the rural glen
　For evermore was gone:
Now, mouldering near the churchyard way,
　All stricken in her pride,
The white rose of the valley lay,
　With an infant by her side.

GLAD WELCOME TO MORN'S DEWY HOURS.

I

GLAD welcome to morn's dewy hours
    The birds warble blithe to the gale,
While the sun shimmers through the green bowers,
    And plays with the stream in the vale;
But, as clouds o'er the heavens come streaming,
    Then silence, with shade, creeps along:
They pass,—and again the woods, gleaming,
    At once wake to sunlight and song.

II.

So I sport, till the storm gathers o'er me;
  Then, pensively hushed in the gloom,
My heart looks around and before me
  For something the shade to illume;
Yet though, folding the wings of my gladness,
  I'm mute in the hurricane's howl,
Thou com'st, through the gloomiest sadness,
  A sunbeam of joy to my soul.

III.

Fair star of remembrance, endearing,
  Still lend me thy brilliant ray,
My wanderings chastening and cheering,
  Till life, with its light, fade away;
And, oft as my pathway thou greetest,
  I'll waken my harp-string to thee,
And sing how the brightest and sweetest
  Are always the swiftest to flee.

ALAS! HOW HARD IT IS TO SMILE.

I.

ALAS! how hard it is to smile
    When all within is sad;
And rooted sorrow to beguile
    By mingling with the glad.
The heart that swells with grief disdains
    Pretension's mean alloy,
And feels far less its keenest pains
    Than mockeries of joy.

II.

How few among the thoughtless crowds
   Can tell the jealous care
With which a gentle spirit shrouds
   Its pangs from worldly glare.
The harp of sorrow wooes the touch
   Of sympathy alone;
Its trembling fibres shrink from such
   As cannot feel their tone.

III.

The gay may sport upon the wave
   Of life's untroubled tides,—
Like birds that warble on a grave,
   They dream not what it hides;
But pleasure's wretched masquerade
   Wakes sorrow's keenest throe;—
The saddest look is not so sad
   As the strainèd smile of woe.

YE GALLANT MEN OF ENGLAND.

1.

YE gallant men of England,
  Of noble races bred,
Remember how your fathers
  For liberty have bled;
Stand to your ancient banners,
  In a thousand battles torn—
The banners of Great Britain,
  To a thousand victories borne!

II.

When flags of tyrants, flying,
  Insult the air again,
And freedom's sons are dying
  Upon the bloody plain,
Rush to the gory havoc
  With all your native might,
And carve your way to justice,
  Or perish for the right.

III.

Ye sons of ancient heroes,
  And heirs of England's fame,
Wherever danger threatens
  Be worthy of your name;
And hurl each bold aggressor
  Into his native lair,
To rule the slaves and traitors
  That crawl around him there.

IV.

Though knaves and cowards tremble
  Beneath despotic sway,
And fools to wily tyrants
  Resign, a willing prey,
The race of island lions,
  Bred by the Western main,
The freedom won by battle
  By battle can maintain.

HERE'S TO MY NATIVE LAND.

I.

HERE'S to my native land;
    And here's to the heathery hills,
Where the little birds sing on the blooming
    boughs,
    To the dancing moorland rills.

II.

Oh, there is a pleasant cot,
    And it stands by a spreading tree,
Where a kind old face has looked from the door
    Full many a time for me;—

III.

On the slope of a flowery dell,
    And hard by a rippling brook;
And it's oh for a peep at the chimney-top,
    Or a glint of the chimney nook!

IV.

And there is a still churchyard,
    Where many an old friend lies;
And I fain would sleep in my native ground
    At last, when they close my eyes.

V.

When summer days were fine,
    The lads of the fold and I
Have roved the moors, till the harvest moon
    Has died in the morning sky.

VI.

Oh, it's sweet in the leafy woods
On a sunny summer's day;
And I wish I was helping yon moorland lads
To tumble their scented hay!

VII.

Though many a pleasant nook
In many a land I've seen,
I'd wander back to my own green hills,
If the wide world lay between.

VIII.

They say there's bluer skies
Across the foaming sea:—
Each man that is born has a land of his own,
And this is the land for me!

WHAT MAKES YOUR LEAVES FALL DOWN?

1.

WHAT makes your leaves fall down,
    Ye drooping autumn flowers?
What makes your green go brown,
    Ye fading autumn bowers?
Oh, thou complaining gale,
    That wand'rest sad and lone,
What sorrows swell the tale
    Of that funereal moan?

II.

Have ye felt love like mine,
 And met with like return,
That ye do thus decline,
 And thus appear to mourn?
Ah, no! content, methinks,
 Ye glide into decay,
As gentle evening sinks,
 At close of summer day.

III.

Fall down, ye leafy bowers!
 And drift upon the gales;
Fade on, ye sleepy flowers!
 It is my heart that wails;
Blow on, thou quiet wind!
 It was a fancied moan—
The echo of a mind
 That feels its pleasure gone.

WHEN DROWSY DAYLIGHT.

I.

WHEN drowsy daylight's drooping e'e
    Closes o'er the fading lea,—
When evening hums his vesper-song,
And twinkling dews the meadow throng,
    I'll come to meet thee, Mary!

II.

The lazy hours refuse to fly;
As glaring day goes creeping by,
I count each moment with a sigh,
Until the hour of shade steals nigh,
    That brings me to my Mary!

III.

The flower is dear unto the lea,
The blossom to the parent tree:—
Thou'rt more than flower and leaf to me—
This heart of mine, by love of thee,
    Must bloom or wither, Mary.

IV.

The summer woods are waving fair;
The cowslip scents the evening air;
The small bird woos its mate to share
Its little nest and loving care:—
    Oh, be my own, my Mary!

MARY.

I.

MY Mary is the queen of girls!
    Cupid's archers round her play,
And bivouac among the curls
    Which her gentle head array!

II.

Her modest glances to and fro—
    Ah, little knows she how they win!—
Would draw an angel down below,
    Or woo the fall'n to heaven again.

III.

The fairest form that ever played
    A poet's sweetest dreams among,
Was not so lovely as the maid
    That wakes this heart of mine to song.

IV

Oh, Mary, such a love as mine
    Idolatry can never be:—
The very altar is divine
    That owns so much of heaven as thee

OH! HAD SHE BEEN A LOWLY MAID.

1.

OH! had she been a lowly maid
    That stole this heart of mine,
She would have filled the humblest shade
    With radiance divine:—
The moon of beauty's starry skies,
    She glides serenely fair,
Absorbing in her gleaming eyes
    The brightest planet there.

11.

Oh! were she but a flower of spring
　Upon the dewy lea,
To watch its lovely blossoming
　My heart's delight would be;
And when its leaves began to fade,
　Their fading I would moan;
And treasure up its sacred dust
　To mingle with my own.

THE OLD BARD'S WELCOME HOME.

BRING me a goblet of drink divine,
    To welcome a minstrel friend of mine!
Enfranchised from the dreary crowd,
That wrapt his spirit like a shroud,
Once more he climbs the moorlands dun,
And hears his native rindles run;
Through pleasant vales he takes his way,
Where wild-flowers with the waters play;

And listens with enchanted mind
As wizard voices in the wind
Sing of his darling native earth,
The rude, the true, unconquered north!
His native dales, his native streams—
The angels of his exile-dreams—
Each dingle green, each breezy height,
Awakes his spirit to delight.
Oh, welcome to the sweet old hills!
The mossy crags, and tinkling rills—
To field, and wood, and moorland glen,
Welcome, welcome home again!

Well may the pleasant summer air
Fondly play with thy silver hair;
Well may the brooklet's ripples clear
Leap as thy footsteps wander near;
Well may the wild-flowers on the lea,
Nodding their pretty heads to thee,

Scatter abroad their sweetest sweet,
Their fond old poet friend to meet;—
They've waited, and have listened long,
For thee, oh, white-haired son of song!

Though tempests rage and clouds are black,
The sun keeps on his glorious track,
Serenely shining, to the west,
And, grandly smiling, sinks to rest.
Thy task, old bard, is nearly done:
Oh, may the evening coming on,
Long lingering sweetly round thy way,
Close like a cloudless summer day!

OH! COME ACROSS THE FIELDS!

I.

NOW, from dreary winter's dream awaking,
    Sweet nature robes herself to meet the spring;
Hark, how the blithesome birds are making
    Among the trees their songs of welcoming!
    Oh, come across the fields, my love,
        And through the woods with me;
    As nature moves toward the spring,
    So moves my heart to thee, my love,
        So moves my heart to thee!

II.

See, from their silent shelters sweetly peeping,
　The budding wild-flowers steal with timid glee;
See the soft fresh verdure, gently creeping,
　Is mantling over the delighted lea!
　　Then come across the fields, my love,
　　　And through the woods with me;
　　As nature moves toward the spring,
　　So moves my heart to thee, my love,
　　　So moves my heart to thee!

III.

Oh! listen, love; it is the throstle's carol,
　In yonder elm-tree ringing loud and clear;—
"First come the buds, and then the bonny blossom—
　The golden summer time will soon be here!"
　　Then come across the fields, my love,
　　　And through the woods with me;
　　As nature moves toward the spring,
　　So moves my heart to thee, my love,
　　　So moves my heart to thee.

IV.

My heart is like a flowerless winter wild,
  Where tuneless joy sits lone, with folded wing,
Until thy beauty comes, enchantress mild,
  To melt the gloom, and make the flowers spring!
    Oh, shine upon my longing heart,
      And I thy charms will sing,
      For thy sweet re-appearing
    Is like another spring, my love,
      Is like another spring!

OH! WEAVE A GARLAND FOR MY BROW.

1.

OH! weave a garland for my brow,
    Of roses and of rue;
For once I loved a bonny lass,—
    Alas, she was not true!
But when she slighted all my grief,
    I knew that grief was vain,
And I hid the wound that pained my heart,
    Until it healed again.

II.

Then, gentle lover, pine no more,—
  Thy tenderness is blind;
Sighing to one whose heart is cold
  Will never make her kind.
Go, take some comfort to thy breast—
  The world is fair to see—
And on some genial bosom rest
  Whose pulses beat for thee.

TO THE SPRING WIND.

I.

SWEET minstrel of the scented spring,
  Ten thousand silver bells,
To welcome thee, are all a-swing,
  Upon the dewy fells:
To sing with thee, I should be fain,
  Thou harper blithe and free!
But love has bound me with a chain,
  That wrings the heart of me.

11.

Oh, hasten to my love, and tell
    Her how she makes me pine;
And ask her if she thinks it well
    To slight a heart like mine;
For if my suit her scorn doth move,
    It shall no longer be,—
Although I know she's made for love,
    And I wish that she loved me.

NIGHTFALL.

I.

THE green leaves answer to the night-wind's sigh,
And dew-drops winking, on the meadows lie;
The sun's gone down
O'er the drowsy town;
And the brooks are singing to the listening moon.

II.

The soft wind whispers on its moody way;
The plumy woodlands in the moonlight play;
Night's tapers gleam
In the gliding stream;
Heaven's eyes are watching while the earth doth dream.

III.

The lovely light that dwells in woman's eyes,
Softly curtained by the fringed lids lies;
    Sleep's Lethean hand
    Waves o'er the land,
And the weary toiler to his shelter hies.

IV.

Old nurse, whose lullaby can soothe them all,
Oh, hap them kindly in thy downy pall!
    They've gone astray
    On life's rough way;
But, rest them; rest them for another day.

V.

The living, sleeping in their warm beds lie;
The dead are sleeping in the churchyard nigh;
    The mild moon's beam
    O'er all doth stream,
And life and death appear a mingling dream.

VI.

Decay, that in my very breath doth creep,
Thou surely art akin to this soft sleep,
    That shews the way
    To a bed of clay,
Whose wakeless slumbers close the mortal day.

VII.

And thus, with ceaseless roll, time's silent wave
Lands me each night upon a mimic grave,
    Whose soft repose
    Hints, at life's close,—
Death's fleets are cruising where life's current flows.

TO A YOUNG LADY

WHO LENT ME AN OLD BOOK.

I

THIS learned volume doth not tell
   A story so divine,
Nor point a moral half so well
   As that young face of thine.

II.

Thou shouldst have sent a rose to me,
   With morning dew bestarred;
It would have better likened thee,—
   Sweet rosebud of the bard!

III.

But mornings fly, and dewdrops dry,
And many a lovely rose
Is plucked, and thrown neglected by,
Before it fairly blows.

IV.

Sweet maid, thy budding time is fair;
So may thy blooming be;
And never blighting blast of care
Untimely wither thee.

V.

Flower on, in gladness, free from stain,
Until the autumn's past;
And, like a fading rose, retain
Thy sweetness to the last.

POOR TRAVELLERS ALL.

I.

POOR travellers all,
   Both great and small,
How thoughtlessly we play
   In a country
   Of mortality,
Where never a man can stay.

II.

Our birth is but
A starting foot
Upon the fatal road,
   Where Death keeps watch
   O'er life to snatch
The jewel back to God.

III.

Time's sickle reaps,
In restless sweeps,
The harvest of decay;
On every ground
His sheaves are bound,
And garnered in the clay.

IV.

Though hints divine,
In symbols fine,
With warnings strew the way,—
Beseeching us,
And teaching us
The danger of delay,—

V.

We dally still,
With fitful will,
Among delusive joys;

Heeding them not,
Except for sport,
As children play with toys.

VI.

We romp and run
Mad in the sun,
And murmuring at the cloud;
And where's the breast
That seems at rest
Until it's in a shroud?

VII.

Thus glides away
Life's little day,
In giddiness and glooms;
And never a one
Can *feel* it's gone,
Until his bed-time comes.

VIII.

Poor travellers all,
Both great and small,
How thoughtlessly we play,
In a country
Of mortality,
Where never a man can stay.

THE DYING ROSE.

I.

BROWN Autumn sings his anthem drear
   O'er Summer's waning pride;
And the water-lily to its bier
   Droops by the brooklet side:
The hour has come, my floral gem,
   That beckons thee away
To join these relics of the bower
   In neighbourly decay.

II.

I saw thy bud, with orient tip,
   Peep forth in beauty rare,
When dewdrops thronged thy blushing lip—
   Thou sweetheart of the air!

But brief, alas, the charm it wrought
    In this delighted eye;
For, 'twas unmingled with a thought
    That thou wert doomed to die.

III.

The golden sunshine smiled to see
    How beautiful it grew;
Rich with its perfume, o'er the lea
    The whispering breezes flew;
The wild bee well might linger long
    Within those rosy folds,—
'Twas there he purchased, for a song,
    The sweetest wealth he holds.

IV.

But Summer's golden glory's o'er;
    All nature seems to moan:
Both leaf and flower have had their hour,
    And home again are gone;

The greenwood's tresses, fallen away,
　　Upon the ground are laid:
And chill winds in the sear leaves play
　　The requiem of the dead.

v.

Not long, at best, thou fading flower,
　　Has man to stay behind;
Cold death may still at any hour
　　The fever of his mind;
May check his frets of joy and grief,
　　Extinguish all his pride,
And lay him, like a blighted leaf,
　　To moulder at thy side.

vi.

But go thy way; 'twas ever so
　　With what's beneath the sky;
We do not all so sweetly grow,
　　Though we as surely die:

Companions in a graveward throng
    Upon a rugged way,
Where trouble cannot keep us long,
    Though joy may never stay.

VII.

Go, rest in peace thy weary head
    The chilling winter through;
New spring shall cheer thy lonely bed,
    And wake thy life anew:
So thou, my soul, shalt rise again,
    To breathe a purer breath,
In climes beyond the fatal chain
    That binds this realm of death.

LINES.

OH! whatever betide thee,
   Thou need not despair;
Where conscience doth guide thee
   Thy safety is there.

If fortune delight thee,
   Beware its alloy;
And should it despite thee,
   Endure it with joy.

For, to win its caressing's
   A dangerous gain;
And Heaven's best blessings
   Are hidden in pain.

While youth and health bless thee,
    Remember the day
When mourners shall dress thee
    To sleep in the clay.

Do good unto all men,
    Contented, unknown,
Expecting thy payment
    From Heaven alone.

THE MAN OF THE TIME.

I.

He is a sterling nobleman
    Who lives the truth he knows;
Who dreads the slavery of sin,
    And fears no other foes.

II.

Who scorns the folly of pretence;
    Whose mind from cant is free;
Who values men for worth and sense,
    And hates hypocrisy.

III.

Who glows with love that's free from taint;
    Whose heart is kind and brave;
Who feels that he was neither meant
    For tyrant nor for slave.

IV.

Who loves the ground, where'er he roam,
    That's trod by human feet,
And strives to make the world a home
    Where peace and justice meet.

V.

Whose soul to clearer heights can climb,
    Above the shows of things,—
Cleaving the mortal bounds of time
    On meditative wings.

VI.

Malice can never mar his fame;
    A heaven-crowned king is he;—
His robe, a pure immortal aim;
    His throne, eternity.

THE WANDERER'S HYMN.

I.

HAPPY the heart that's simply pure;
    Happy the heart that's nobly brave;
Happy is he that shuns the lure
    That winds like death round folly's slave.

II.

Wandering in the worldly throng,
    The dust of earth still keeps us blind;—
The judgment's weak, the passions strong,
    The will is fitful as the wind.

III.

Disguised in joy's deceitful beams,
    A thousand dancing meteors ply
About our path the demon-schemes,
    That glitter only to destroy.

IV.

Who can we ask for aid but Thee,
    Our only friend, our only guide?
What other counsellor have we?
    Where else, oh! where, can we abide?

V.

Oh! hear and help us while we pray,
    And travel with us all the way!
Oh! hold our hands, and be our stay!
    Oh! set us right whene'er we stray!

ALONE, UPON THE FLOWERY PLAIN.

I.

ALONE, upon the flowery plain
I rove, in solitary pain,
Looking around the silent lea
For something I shall never see.

II.

Yon hedge-row blossoms as before,
And roses shade yon cottage door;
But oh, I miss the tresses fair,
And eyes that beamed with welcome there.

III.

The streamlet runs in rippling pranks,
Kissing the wild flower on its banks;
But I am lonely on the shore,
To which my love returns no more.

IV.

The lark aloft in sunny air
Carols, as if my love was there;
And the wind goes by with mournful sound,
Murmuring, "No more, on mortal ground."

LIFE'S TWILIGHT.

1.

NOW silver threads begin to shine
  Among my wasting hair,
And down the slope of life's decline
  I thoughtfully repair.
The fire that once was in mine eyes
  Has dimmed its fervid ray,
And every hour of life that flies,
  Is stealing light away.

Oh, let me, with untroubled breast,
    A while in shadow lie,
Before I lay me down to rest,
    And bid the world "Good bye."

II.

With Time, that wrestler old and grim,
    I've had a gallant round;
But ah, there's little chance with him
    Who bringeth all to ground.
Although the world still rolleth on
    Its merry, motley, way,
My little part of life is done,
    Except to watch the play.
Then, let me, with untroubled breast,
    A while in shadow lie,
Before I lay me down to rest,
    And bid the world "Good bye."

III.

In youth, to pleasure's lightest trill,
  My heart leaped blithe and free;
Now, she may play what tune she will,
  It is not so with me;
For though a smile may sometimes steal
  Across my furrowed brow,
My joys are all akin, I feel,
  To contemplation now.
Then, let me, with untroubled breast,
  A while in shadow lie,
Before I lay me down to rest,
  And bid the world " Good bye."

CHRISTMAS MORNING.

I.

COME all you weary wanderers,
  Beneath the wintry sky,
This day forget your worldly cares,
  And lay your sorrows by;
    Awake, and sing;
    The church bells ring;
  For this is Christmas morning!

II.

With grateful hearts salute the morn,
   And swell the streams of song,
That laden with great joy are borne,
   The willing air along;
     The tidings thrill
     With right good will;
   For this is Christmas morning!

III.

We'll twine the fresh green holly wreath,
   And make the yule-log glow;
And gather gaily underneath
   The winking mistletoe;
     All blithe and bright
     By the glad fire-light;
   For this is Christmas morning!

IV.

Come, sing the carols old and true,
    That mind us of good cheer,
And, like a heavenly fall of dew,
    Revive the drooping year;
        And fill us up
        A wassail-cup;
    For this is Christmas morning!

V.

To all poor souls we'll strew the feast,
    With willing heart and free;
One Father owns us, and, at least,
    To-day we'll brothers be;
        Away with pride,
        This holy tide;
    For it is Christmas morning!

VI.

So now God bless us one and all
    With hearts and hearthstones warm;
And may he prosper great and small,
    And keep us out of harm;
        And teach us still,
        His sweet good-will,
This merry Christmas morning!

SONGS

IN THE LANCASHIRE DIALECT.

COME WHOAM TO THY CHILDER AN' ME.

1.

AW'VE just mended th' fire wi' a cob;
    Owd Swaddle has brought thi new shoon;
There's some nice bacon-collops o'th hob,
    An a quart o' ale posset i'th oon;
Aw've brought thi top-cwot, does ta know,
    For th' rain's comin' deawn very dree;
An' th' har'stone's as white as new snow;—
    Come whoam to thi childer an' me.

II.

When aw put little Sally to bed,
  Hoo cried, 'cose her feyther were n't theer;
So, aw kissed th' little thing, an' aw said
  Thae'd bring her a ribbin fro th' fair;
An' aw gav her her doll, an' some rags,
  An' a nice little white cotton bo';
An' aw kissed her again; but hoo said
  At hoo wanted to kiss *thee* an' o'.

III.

An' Dick, too, aw'd sich wark wi' him,
  Afore aw could get him up stairs;
Thae towd him thae'd bring him a drum,
  He said, when he're sayin' his prayers;
Then he looked i' my face, an' he said,
  " Has th' boggarts taen houd o' my dad?"
An' he cried till his e'en were quite red;—
  He likes thee some weel, does yon lad!

IV.

At th' lung-length, aw geet 'em laid still;
    An' aw hearken't folk's feet at went by;
So aw iron't o' my clooas reet weel,
    An' aw hanged 'em o' th maiden to dry;
When aw'd mended thi stockin's an' shirts,
    Aw sit deawn to knit i' my cheer,
An' aw rayley did feel rather hurt,—
    Mon, aw'm *one-ly* when theaw art n't theer.

V.

"Aw've a drum an' a trumpet for Dick;
    Aw've a yard o' blue ribbin for Sal;
Aw've a book full o' babs; an' a stick,
    An' some 'bacco an' pipes for mysel;
Aw've brought thee some coffee an' tay,—
    Iv thae'll *feel* i' my pocket, thae'll *see;*
An' aw bought thee a new cap to-day,—
    But, aw olez bring summat for *thee!*"

VI.

"God bless tho, my lass; aw'll go whoam,
  An' aw'll kiss thee an' th' chiider o' reawnd;
Thae knows, that wheerever aw roam,
  Aw'm fain to get back to th' owd greawnd.
Aw can do wi' a crack o'er a glass;
  Aw can do wi' a bit ov a spree;
But aw've no gradely comfort, my lass,
  Except wi' yon childer an' thee!"

WHAT AILS THEE, MY SON ROBIN

1.

WHAT ails thee, my son Robin?
  My heart is sore for thee;
Thi cheeks are grooin' thinner,
  An' th' leet has laft thi e'e;
Theaw trails abeawt so lonesome,
  An' looks so pale at morn;
God bless tho, lad, aw'm soory
  To see tho so forlorn!

II.

Thi fuutstep's sadly awter't,—
   Aw used to know it weel,—
Neaw, arto fairy-strucken;
   Or, arto gradely ill?
Or, hasto bin wi' th' witches
   I'th cloof, at deep o'th neet?
Come, tell mo, Robin, tell mo,
   For summat isn't reet!

III.

"Neaw, mother, dunnut fret yo;
   Aw am not like mysel;
But, 'tisn't lung o'th feeorin'
   That han to do wi'th' dule;
There's nought at thus could daunt mo,
   I'th cloof, by neet nor day;—
It's yon blue een o' Mary's:—
   They taen my life away!"

IV.

"Aw deawt aw done wi' comfort
  To th' day that aw mun dee,
For th' place hoo sets her fuut on,
  It's fairy greawnd to me;
But oh, it's useless speykin',
  Aw connut ston her pride;
An' when a true heart's breykin',
  It's very hard to bide!"

V.

Neaw, God be wi' tho, Robin;
  Just let her have her way;
Hoo'll never meet thy marrow,
  For mony a summer day;
Aw're just same wi' thi feyther,
  When first he spoke to me;
So go thi ways an' whistle,
  An' th' lass'll come to thee!

GOD BLESS THESE POOR FOLK!

1.

GOD bless these poor folk that are strivin'
By means that are honest an' true,
For summat to keep 'em alive in
This world that we're scramblin' through;
As th' life ov a mon's full o' feightin',
A mortal that wants to do fair,
Should never be grudged ov his heytin',
For th' hardest o' th battle's his share.
Chorus.—As th' life ov a mon.

II.

This world's kin to trouble; i' th best on't,
  There's mony sad changes come reawnd;
We wandern abeawt to find rest on't,
  An' th' worm yammers for us i' th greawnd;
May he that'll wortch while he's able,
  Be never long hungry nor dry;
'An' th' childer at sit at his table,—
  God bless 'em wi' plenty, say I.
    Chorus.—As th' life ov a mon.

III.

An' he that can feel it a pleasur'
  To leeten misfortin an' pain,—
May his pantry be olez full measur',
  To cut at, and come to again;
May God bless his cup and his cupbort,
  A theawsan for one that he gives;
An' his heart be a bumper o' comfort,
  To th' very last minute he lives!
    Chorus.—As th' life ov a mon.

IV.

An' he that scorns ale to his victual
    Is welcome to let it alone;
There's some can be wise with a little,
    An' some that are foolish wi' noan;
An' some are so quare i' their natur,
    That nought wi' their stomachs agree;
But he that would liefer drink wayter,
    Shall never be stinted by me.
        Chorus.—As th' life ov a mon.

V.

One likes to see hearty folk wortchin',
    An' weary folk havin' a rest;
One likes to yer poor women singin'
    To th' little things laid o' their breast:
Good cooks are my favourite doctors;
    Good livers my parsons shall be;
An' ony poor craytur at's clemmin,
    May come have a meawthful wi' me.
        Chorus.—As th' life ov a mon.

VI.

Owd Time,—he's a troublesome codger,—
   Keeps nudgin' us on to decay,
An' whispers, " Yo're nobbut a lodger ;
   Get ready for goin' away ; "
Then let's ha' no skulkin' nor sniv'lin',
   Whatever misfortins befo' ;
God bless him that fends for his livin',
   An' houds up his yed through it o' !
       Chorus.—As th' life ov a mon.

COME, MARY, LINK THI ARM I' MINE.

1.

COME, Mary, link thi arm i' mine,
   An' lilt away wi' me;
An' dry that tremblin' drop o' brine
   Fro th' corner o' thi e'e;
Thea knows that cot aside o' th' spring,—
   Come, lass, an' live wi' me,
Aw'll buy tho th' prattist gowden ring
   That ever theaw did see!
Chorus.—Come, Mary, link thi arm i' mine.

II.

My feyther's gan mo forty peawnd
  I' silver an' i' gowd;
An' a bonny bit o' garden greawnd,
  O'th mornin' side o'th' fowd;
An' a honsome Bible, clen an' new,
  To read for days to come;—
There's lyevs for writin' names in, too,
  Like th' owd un at's awhoam.
Chorus.—Come, Mary, link thi arm i' mine.

III.

Eawr Jenny's bin a-buyin' in,
  An' every day hoo brings
Knives an' forks, an' pots; an' irons
  For smoothin' caps an' things;
My gronny's sent a kist o' drawers,
  Sunday clooas to keep;
An' little Fanny's bought a glass,
  Where thee an' me can peep.
Chorus.—Come, Mary, link thi arm i' mine.

IV.

Eawr Tum has sent a bacon-flitch;
    Eawr Jem a load o' coals;
Eawr Charlie's bought some pickters, an'
    He's hanged 'em upo th' woles;
Owd Posy's white-weshed th' cottage through;
    Eawr Matty's made it sweet;
An' Jack's gan me his Jarman flute
    To play by th' fire at neet!
Chorus.—Come, Mary, link thi arm i' mine.

V.

There's cups an' saucers; porritch-pons,
    An' tables, greyt an' smo';
There's brushes, mugs, an' ladin-cans;
    An eight day's clock an' o';
There's a cheer for thee, an' one for me,
    An' one i' every nook;
Thi mother's has a cushion on't—
    It's th' nicest cheer i' th rook.
Chorus.—Come, Mary, link thi arm i' mine.

VI.

My mother's gan me th' four-post bed,
  Wi' curtains to't an' o';
An' pillows, sheets, an' bowsters, too,
  As white as driven snow;
It isn't stuffed wi' fither-deawn,
  But th' flocks are clen an' new;
Hoo says there's honest folk i'th teawn
  That's made a warse un do.
Chorus.—Come, Mary, link thi arm i' mine.

VII.

Aw peeped into my cot last neet;
  It made me hutchin' fain;
A bonny fire were winkin' breet
  I' every window-pane;
Aw marlocked upo th' white hearth-stone,
  An' drummed o'th kettle lid;
An' sung, "My neest is snug an' sweet;
  Aw'll go and fotch my brid!"
Chorus.—Come, Mary, link thi arm i' mine.

CHIRRUP.

I.

YOUNG Chirrup wur a mettled cowt;
  His heart an' limbs wur true;
At foot race, or at wrostlin'-beawt,
  Or aught he buckled to;
At wark or play, reet gallantly
  He laid into his game;
An' he're very fond o' singin'-brids'—
  That's heaw he geet his name.

II.

He're straight as ony pickin'-rod,
    An' limber as a snig;
He're th' heartist cock o' th' village clod,
    At every country rig;
His shinin' e'en wur clear an' blue;
    His face wur frank an' bowd;
An' th' yure abeawt his monly broo
    Wur crispt i' curls o' gowd!

III.

Young Chirrup donned his clinker't shoon,
    An' startin' off to th' fair,
He swore by th' leet o' th harvest moon,
    He'd have a marlock there;
He poo'd a sprig for th' hawthorn-tree,
    That blossomed by the way;—
"Iv ony mon says wrang to me,
    Aw'll tan his hide to-day!"

IV.

Full sorely mony a lass would sigh,
  That chanced to wander near,
An' peep into his e'en, to spy
  Iv love wur lurkin' theer;
So fair an' free he stept o' th green,
  An' trollin' eawt his sung,
Wi' leetsome heart, an' twinklin' e'en,
  Went chirrupin' alung.

V.

Young Chirrup woo'd a village maid,—
  An' hoo wur th' flower ov o',—
Wi' kisses kind, i' th woodlan' shade,
  An' whispers soft an' low;
I' Matty's ear 't wur th' sweetest chime
  That ever mortal sung;
An' Matty's heart beat pleasant time
  To th' music ov his tung.

VI.

Oh, th' kindest mates, this world within,
  Mun ha' their share o' pain;
But, iv this pair could life begin,
  They'd buckle to again;
For, though he're hearty, blunt, an' tough,
  An' Matty sweet and mild,
For three-score year, through smooth and
    rough,
  Hoo led him like a child.

THE DULE'S I' THIS BONNET O' MINE.

I.

THE dule's i' this bonnet o' mine;
    My ribbins'll never be reet;
Here, Mally, aw'm like to be fine,
    For Jamie'll be comin' to-meet;
He met me i'th lone tother day,—
    Aw're gooin' for wayter to th' well,—
An' he begged that aw'd wed him i' May;—
    Bi'th mass, iv he'll let me, aw will.

II.

When he took my two honds into his,
   Good Lord, heaw they trembled between;
An' aw durstn't look up in his face,
   Becose on him seein' my e'en;
My cheek went as red as a rose;—
   There's never a mortal can tell
Heaw happy aw felt; for, thea knows,
   One couldn't ha' axed him theirsel'.

III.

But th' tale wur at th' end o' my tung,—
   To let it eawt wouldn't be reet,—
For aw thought to seem forrud wur wrung;
   So aw towd him aw'd tell him to-neet;
But, Mally, thae knows very weel,—
   Though 'tisn't a thing one should own,—
If aw'd th' pikein' o' th world to mysel',
   Aw'd oather ha' Jamie or noan.

IV.

Neaw, Mally, aw towd tho my mind;
 What would to do iv 't wur thee?
"Aw'd tak him just while he're inclined;
 An' a farrantly bargain he'll be;
For Jamie's as greadly a lad
 As ever stept eawt into th' sun;—
Go, jump at thy chance, an' get wed,
 An' may th' best o' th job when it's done!"

V.

Eh, dear, but it's time to be gwon!
 Aw should'nt like Jamie to wait,—
Aw connut for shame be to soon,
 An' aw wouldn't for th' world be to late;
Aw'm o' ov a tremble to th' heel,—
 Dost think at my bonnet'll do?—
"Be off, lass,—thae looks very weel;—
 He wahts noan o'th bonnet, thae foo!"

TICKLE TIMES.

I

HERE'S Robin looks fyerfully gloomy,
    An' Jamie keeps starin' at th' greawnd,
An' thinkin' o' th table at's empty,
    An' th' little things yammerin' reawnd;
It looks rayther darksome afore us,
    But, keep your hearts eawt o' your shoon,
Though clouds may be getherin' o'er us,
    There's lots o' blue heaven aboon!

II.

But, when a mon's able an' willin',
    An' never a stroke to be had,—
An' clemmin' for want ov a shillin',—
    No wonder that he should be sad;
It troubles his heart to keep seein'
    His little birds feedin' o' th air;
An' it feels very hard to be deein',
    An' never a mortal to care.

III.

This life's sich a quare little travel,—
    A marlock wi' sun an' wi' shade,—
An' then, on a bowster o' gravel,
    They lay'n us i' bed wi' a spade;
It's no use o' peawtin' an' fratchin',—
    As th' whirligig's twirlin' areawnd,
Have at it again; an' keep scratchin'
    As lung as your yed's upo greawnd!

IV.

Iv one could but grope i'th' inside on't
    There's trouble i' every heart;
An' thoose that'n th' biggest o' th pride on't,
    Oft leeten o' th' keenest o' th smart.
Then, lads, as whatever comes to us,
    Let's patiently hondle er share;
For there's mony a fine suit o' clooas,
    That covers a murderin' care.

V.

There's danger i' every station,—
    I' th palace as much as i' th cot;
There's hanker i' every condition,
    An' canker i' every lot;
There's folk that are weary o' livin'
    That never fear't hunger nor cowd;
An' mony a miserly nowmun,
    Has deed ov a surfeit o' gowd.

VI.

One feels, neaw that times are so nippin',
    He gwos to a troublesome schoo,
That slaves like a horse for his livin',
    An' flings it away like a foo ;
But, as pleasur's sometimes a misfortin,
    An' trouble sometimes a good thing,
Though we live'n o'th' floor, same as layrocks,
    We'n go up, like layrocks, to sing !

JAMIE'S FROLIC.

I.

ONE neet aw crope whoam, when my weighvin'
    were o'er,
To brush mo, an' wesh mo, an' fettle my yure;
Then, slingin' abeawt, wi' my heart i' my shoon
Kept tryin' my hond at a bit ov a tune,
    As Mally sit rockin',
    An' darnin' a stockin',
    An' tentin' her bakin' i' th o'on.

II.

Th' chylt were asleep, an' my clooas were reet;
Th' baggin' were ready, an' o' lookin' sweet;
But, aw're mazy, an' nattle, an' fasten't to tell
What the dule it could be that're ailin' mysel',—
    An' it made me so naught,
    That, o' someheaw, aw thought,
"Aw could just like a snap at eawr Mall."

III.

Poor lass! hoo were kinder becose aw were quare;
"Jamie, come sattle thisel' in a cheer;
Thae's looked very yonderly mony a day;
It's grievin' to see heaw thae'rt wearin' away,—
    An' trailin' abeawt,
    Like a hen at's i'th meawt;—
Do, pritho, poo up to thi tay!"

IV.

"Thae wants some new flannels,—thae's getten a
    cowd,—
Thae'rt noather so ugly, my lad, nor so owd,—
But, thae'rt makin' thisel' into nought but a slave,
Wi' weighvin', an' thinkin', an' tryin' to save;—
      Get summat to heyt,
      Or thae'll go eawt o' seet,—
    For thae'rt wortchin' thisel' into th' grave."

V.

Thinks I, "Th' lass's reet, an' aw houd with her wit;"
So, aw said,—for aw wanted to cheer her a bit,—
"Owd crayter, aw've noan made my mind up to dee,—
A frolic 'll just be the physic for me!
      Aw'll see some fresh places,
      An' look at fresh faces,—
    An' go have a bit ov a spree!"

VI.

Then, bumpin' an' splashin' her kettle went deawn;
"I'th name o' good Katty, Jem, wheer arto beawn?
An' what sort o' faces dost want,—con to tell?
Aw deawt thae'rt for makin' a foo o' thisel',—
  The dule may tent th' o'on;
  Iv aw go witheawt shoon,
 Aw'll see where thae gwos to mysel'!"

VII.

Thinks I, "Th' fat's i'th fire,—aw mun make it no wur,—
For there's plenty o' feightin' to do eawt o'th dur,—
So, aw'll talk very prattily to her, as heaw,
Or else hoo'll have houd o' my toppin in neaw;"—
  An', bith leet in her e'en,
  It were fair to be sin
 That hoo're ready to rive me i' teaw.

VIII.

Iv truth mun be towd, aw began to be fain
To study a bit o' my cwortin' again;
So aw said to her, "Mally, this world's rough enoo!
To fo' eawt wi' thoose one likes best, winnut do,—
    It's a very sore smart,
    An' it sticks long i' th heart,"—
An' egad, aw said nought boh what's true!

IX.

Lord, heaw a mon talks when his heart's in his tung!
Aw roos't her, poor lass, an' shewed hoo wur wrung,
Till hoo took mo bith hond, with a tear in her e'e,
An' said, "Jamie, there's nobry as tender as thee!
    Forgi mo, lad, do;
    For aw'm nobbut a foo,—.
An' bide wi' mo, neaw, till aw dee!"

X.

So, we'n bide one another, whatever may come;
For, there's no peace i'th world iv there's no peace
    awhoam;
An' neaw, when a random word gi's her some pain,
Or makes her a little bit crossish i' th grain,
    Sunshine comes back,
    As soon as aw crack
  O' beginning my cwortin' again.

OWD PINDER.

1.

OWD Pinder were a rackless foo,
   An' spent his days i' spreein';
At th' end ov every drinkin-do,
   He're sure to crack o' deein';
" Go, sell my rags, an' sell my shoon;
   Aw's never live to trail 'em;
My ballis-pipes are eawt o' tune,
   An' th' wynt begins to fail 'em!"

II.

"Eawr Matty's very fresh an' yung;—
   'T would any mon bewilder;—
Hoo'll wed again afore its lung,
   For th' lass is fond o' childer;
My bit o' brass'll fly,—yo'n see,—
   When th' coffin-lid has screened me,—
It gwos again my pluck to dee,
   An' lyev her wick beheend me."

III.

"Come, Matty, come, an' cool my yed;
   Aw'm finish'd, to my thinkin';"
Hoo happed him nicely up, an' said,
   "Its nought i' th world but drinkin';"—
"Nay, nay," said he, "my fuddle's done;
   We're partin' one fro tother;
Just promise me that when aw'm gwon,
   Thea'll never wed another!"

IV.

"Th' owd tale," said hoo, an' laft her stoo;
  "Its rayley past believin';
Thee think o' th world thea'rt goin' to,
  An' lyev this here to th' livin';
What use to me can dyed folk be?
  Thae's kilt thisel' wi' spreein';
An' iv that's o' thae wants wi' me,
  Get forrud wi' thi deein'!"

V.

He scrat his yed, he rubbed his e'e,
  An' then he donned his breeches;
"Eawr Matty gets as fause," said he,
  "As one o' Pendle witches;
Iv ever aw'm to muster wit,
  It mun be now or never;
Aw think aw'll try to live a bit;
  It winnut do to lyev her!"

COME, JAMIE, LET'S UNDO THI SHOON.

I.

COME, Jamie, let's undo thi shoon;
    An' don summat dry o' thi feet;
Thea's bin amung th' sheawer up an' deawn;
    Aw'm fleyed at thi stockin's are weet;
An', here, wi' my yung uns i'th neest,
    Aw bin heark'nin' to th' patterin' rain,
An' longing for th' wanderin' brid
    To comfort my spirits again.

II.

Just when it were peltin' at th' height,
"Aw'll ston it no longer," said I;
For, rayley, it didn't look reet
To keawer under cover so dry;
So, though it were rainin' like mad,
Aw thought—for my heart gav a swell,—
"Come deawn asto will, but yon lad
Shall not have it o' to hissel'!"

III.

So whippin' my bucket i' th rain,
Aw ga' th' bits o' windows a swill;
An', though aw geet weet to my skin,
Aw're better content wi' mysel';
But, theaw stons theer smilin' o' th' floor,
Like a sun-fleawer drippin' wi' weet;
Eh, Jamie, theaw knowsn't, aw'm sure,
Heaw fain aw'm to see tho to-neet!

IV.

Why, lass; what's a sheawer to me?
   Aw've plenty o' sun i' my breast,
My wark keeps me hearty an' free,
   An' gi's me a relish for rest;
Aw'm noan made o' sugar nor saut,
   That melts wi' a steepin' o' rain;
An', as for my jacket,—it's nought,—
   Aw'll dry it by th' leet o' thi e'en!

V.

So, sit tho deawn close by my side,—
   Aw'm full as a cricket wi' glee;
Aw'm trouble't wi' nothin' but pride,
   An' o' on it owin' to thee;
My trim little pattern o' wives;—
   Come, give a poor body a kiss!
Aw wish every storm ov er lives
   May end up as nicely as this!

TH' GOBLIN PARSON.

I.

TH' wynt wur still i' th' shade o' th' hill,
  An' stars began o' glowin'
I' th fadin' leet, one summer neet,
  When dew wur softly foin';
Wi' weary shanks, by primrose banks,
  Where rindlin' weet wur shinin',
Aw whistle't careless, wanderin' slow,
  Toward my cot inclinin'.

II.

Through th' woodlan' green aw tooted keen,
    For th' little window winkin';—
Th' stars may shine, they're noan as fine
    As Matty's candle blinkin';
O'er th' rosy hedge aw went to th' ridge
    O' th' lonesome-shaded plantin',
To get another blink o' th' leet
    That set my heart a-pantin'.

III.

Then deawn bith well ith' fairy-dell,
    Wi' trees aboon it knittin',
Where, near an' fur, ther nowt astur
    But bats i'th eawl-leet flittin';
An' fyerful seawnds that russle't reawnd
    I' mony a goblin-flitter,
As swarmin' dark to flaysome wark
    They flew wi' hellish titter.

IV.

There, reet anent aw geet a glent
  At brought a shiver o'er me,
For, fair i'th track ther summat black
  Coom creepin' on afore me;
It wur not clear, but it wur theer,
  Wi' th' gloomy shadow blendin',
Neaw black an' slim, neaw grey an' grim,
  Wi' noather side nor endin'.

V.

Cowd drops wur tremblin' o' my broo,
  As there aw stoode belated;—
Aw durstn't turn, aw durstn't goo,
  But shut my e'en, an' waited;
An' just as aw began to pray,
  There coom fro' th' creepin' spectre
A friendly seawnd that said, "Well James!"—
  'T wur nowt but th' village rector.

VI.

"Well, James," said he, "I'm fain to see
   Yor pew so weel attended,
But then, yo shouldn't fo' asleep
   Afore my sarmon's ended;
To dreawsy ears it's useless quite
   To scatter holy teychin';
Heaw leets yo dunnot bring some snuff,
   An' tak it while I'm preychin'."

VII.

"Well well," said aw, "there's mony a way
   O' keepin' e'en fro' closin',
A needle would may th' body wake,
   An' th' spirit still be dozin';
But this receipt would set it reet,
   Iv th' mixture were a warm un,—
Yo' m' get some stingin' gospel-snuff,
   An' put it into th' sarmon."

VIII.

He stare't like mad, but th' good owd lad
   Then grip't my hond, warm-hearted,
An' said, "Yo're reet, yo're reet—good neet!"
   An' that wur heaw we parted.
It touched my heart, an' made it smart,
   He spoke so mild and pratty;—
Aw blest him as he walked away,
   An' then went whoam to Matty.

WHILE TAKIN' A WIFT O' MY PIPE.

1.

WHILE takin' a wift o' my pipe, 'tother neet,
    A thowt trickled into my pate,
That sulkin' becose everything isn't sweet,
    Is nobbut a foolish consate;
Iv mon had bin made for a bit of a spree,
    An' th' world were a marlockin' schoo,
Wi' nothin' but heytin', an' drinkin', an' glee,
    An' haliday gam to go through,
        He'd sicken afore
        His frolic were o'er,
    An' feel he'd bin born for a foo.

II.

Poor crayter, he's o' discontentment an' deawt,
　Whatever his fortin may be;
He's just like a chylt at goes yeawlin' abeawt,
　" Eawr Johnny's moor traycle nor me;"
One minute he's trouble't, next minute he's fain,
　An' then, they're so blended i' one,
It's hard to tell whether he's laughin' through pain,
　Or whether he's cryin' for fun;—
　　He stumbles, an' grumbles,
　　An' struggles, an' juggles,—
　He capers a bit,—an' he's gone.

III.

It's wise to be humble i' prosperous ways,
　For trouble may chance to be nee;
It's wise for to struggle wi' sorrowful days,
　Till sorrow breeds sensible glee;
He's rich that, contented wi' little, lives weel,
　An' nurses his little to moor;

He's weel off that's rich, iv he nobbut can feel
 He's brother to those that are poor;
  An' to him that does fair,
  Though his livin' be bare,
Some comfort shall ever be sure.

IV.

We'n nobbut a lifetime a-piece here below,
 An' th' lungest is very soon spent;
There's summat aboon measur's cuts for us o',
 An' th' most on 'em nobbut a fent;
Lung or short, rough or fine, little matter for that,
 We'n make th' best o' th' stuff till its done,
An' when it leets eawt to get rivven a bit,
 Let's darn it as weel as we con;
  When th' order comes to us
  To doff these owd clooas,
There'll surely be new ones to don.

GOD BLESS THI SILVER YURE.

I.

JONE, lad, though thi hond's
  Like reawsty iron to feel,
There's very few i'th lond
  Aw like to gripe as weel;
Thae'll never dee i'th dumps
  Becose o' bein' poor,
Thae good owd king o' trumps,—
  God bless thi silver yure !

II.

Come, poo a cheer to th' hob,
    An rest thi weary shanks,
An' dunnot fret thi nob
    Wi' fortin an' her pranks;
These folk at's preawd an' rich
    May tremble at her freawn,—
They'n further far nor sich
    As thee to tumble deawn.

III.

Thae needn't long for wine,
    Nor dainties rich an' rare,
For sich a life as thine
    Can sweeten simple fare;
Contented wi' thi meal
    Thae's wit enough to know
That daisies liven weel
    Where tulips connot grow.

IV.

An' though thi clooas are rough,
    An' gettin' very owd,
They onswer'n weel enough
    To keep thi limbs fro cowd;
A foo would pine away
    I' sich a suit as thine,
But, thea'rt the stuff to may
    A' fustian jacket fine.

V.

A tatter't clout may lap
    A very noble prize;
A king may be, by hap,
    A beggar i' disguise;
When tone has laft his feast,
    An' tother done his crust,
Then, who can tell, at last,
    Which is th' finest dust!

VI.

An' though thy share o' life
  May seem a losin' game,
Thae's striven fair ith strife,
  An' kept a decent aim;
No meawse-nooks i' thi mind,
  Nor malice i' thi breast,
Thae's still bin true an' kind,
  An' trusted 'fate wi' th' rest.

VII.

Through trouble, toil, an' wrung,
  Whistlin' at thi wark,
Thae's wrostle't life so lung,
  Thi limbs are gettin' stark;
But sich a heart as thine's
  A never-failin' friend;
It cheers a mon's decline,
  An' keeps it sweet to th' end.

VIII.

Th' banner 'll soon be furled,
    An' then they 'n ha' to tell,
" He travelled th' dirty world,
    An' never soil't hissel';
An' when aw come to dee,
    An' death has taen his tow,
Aw hope to leet o' thee,—
    God bless thy snowy pow!

MARGIT'S COMIN'.

I.

EH, Sam, whatever doesto myen;
    Aw see thae'rt theer i'th nook again;
Where aw've a gill thae's nine or ten,—
    Has somebry laft a fortin?
Aw wonder heaw a mon can sit
An' waste his bit o' wage an' wit;
Iv aw're thy wife, aw'd make tho flit,
    Wi' little time to start in.

II.

But, stop; yor Margit's up i'th teawn;
Aw yerd her ax for thee at the Creawn;
An', just meet neaw, aw scamper't deawn;
    It's true as aught i'th Bible;
Thae knows yor Margit weel, ov owd,
Bith mass, her tung makes me go cowd,
Sin th' time hoo broke my nose i'th fowd,
    Wi' the end o' th' porritch thible.

III.

It's ten to one hoo'll co' in here,
An' poo tho eawt o' th' corner cheer;
So, sit nar th' dur, where th' runnin's clear;—
    Aw'll keep my e'en o' th' window;
Neaw, mind te hits, an' when aw sheawt,
Be limber-legged, an' lammas eawt,—
An', though hoo'll not believe, aw deawt,—
    Aw'll swear aw've never sin tho.

IV

Aw'll bite my tung,—aw will, bith mon,
An' plug my ears up, till hoo's gone;
A grooin' tree could hardly ston
    A savage woman flytin';
Eh, dear, iv folk were o' i'th mind
To make their bits o' booses kind,
There'd be less wanderin' eawt to find
    A corner to be quiet in.

V.

It's nearly three o'clock bith chime;
This ale o' Jone's is very prime;
Aw'll keawer me deawn till baggin-time,
    An' have a reech o' bacco;
Thae's yerd abeawt Owd Clinker lad
An' Liltin' Jenny gettin' wed;
An' Collop gooin' wrang i' th. yed,—
    But, that's not mich to crack o'.

VI.

There's news that chaps that wore a creawn,
Are getting powler't up an' deawn;
They're puncin' 'em fro teawn to teawn,
    Like fuut-bo's in a pastur;
Yon Garibaldi's gan 'em silk;
Th' owd brid; he fairly made 'em swilk,
An' neaw, they sen he's sellin' milk,
    To raise new clooas for Ayster.

VII.

There's some are creepin' eawt o' th' slutch;
An' some are gettin' deawn i'th ditch;
Bith mass, aw never knew o' sich
    A world for tickle fortin';
They're gooin' groanin' eawt o' seet;
They're comin' cryin' into the leet;
But, howd,—aw yerd o' Monday neet,
    A crack abeawt a cwortin'.

VIII.

Poo up ; aw'll tell it iv aw con ;—
Thae knows that bow-legged railway mon,—
But, heigh,—aw see yor Margit yon,—
    Hoo's comin' like a racer !
Some foo has put her upo' th' track ;
Hoo'll be i'th heawse in hauve a crack ;
Be sharp ; an' mizzle eawt at th' back,—
    Egad, aw dar not face her !

In one vol. 12mo, price 5s.

The Original:

A Collection of Papers by the late THOMAS WALKER of Manchester.

Nearly ready, uniform with this Volume,

Lancashire Ballads

From Various Sources.

Collected and re-arranged by EDWIN WAUGH.

EDWIN SLATER, MANCHESTER.

www.ingramcontent.com/pod-product-compliance
Lightning Source LLC
Chambersburg PA
CBHW020846160426
43192CB00007B/811